Dearest Cla...
Just have to
remind you of. your
short stay in Cape Town
+ if you ever want to
know where I am
just look in
here!
love
Fiona

BEAUTIFUL
Cape Town

BEAUTIFUL
Cape Town

Cape Town, legislative capital of South Africa, is by far the country's oldest urban centre: it began life in the mid-17th century as a replenishment outpost for the Indies-bound fleets of Holland's great maritime empire. The central metropolitan area fills the amphitheatre formed by the majestic Table Mountain massif and its two flanking peaks; suburbs extend both north-wards, over the low-lying, sandy plain known as the Cape Flats, and southwards into the scenically lovely Cape Peninsula.

Kapstadt: Einst versorgte die ehemalige Proviantstation, gegründet Mitte des 17ten Jahrhunderts, die Schiffe der mächtigen holländischen Handelsflotte en route nach Indien, heute ist Kapstadt legislatorische Hauptstadt und bei weitem die älteste Stadt des Landes. Der Stadtkern liegt wie in einem Amphitheater, umrahmt vom majestätischen Tafelberg, Löwenkopf und Teufelsberg. Weit erstrecken sich die Vororte über die sandige Kapebene nach Norden, und in den malerischen Süden der Halbinsel.

La Ville du Cap, la capitale législative de l'Afrique du Sud, est de loin le centre urbain le plus ancien du pays: c'est au 17ième siècle qu'elle a débuté comme poste colonial de réapprovi-sionnement des flottes du grand empire maritime Hollandais en route pour les Indes. Le massif de la Montagne de la Table majestueuse ainsi que les deux pics sur ses flancs s'élèvent en amphitéâtre autour de la métropole centrale; les faubourgs s'éten-dent au nord, sur un terrain bas sableux qu'on appelle les Cape Flats et au sud à travers la belle Péninsule spectaculaire du Cap.

🇬🇧 *The elegant Heerengracht thoroughfare (opposite) runs from the harbour towards the mountain, changing its name to Adderley Street –Cape Town's main shopping route–at about the halfway mark. Left: The massive, stone-walled Castle, a fortress completed in 1676 and today South Africa's oldest occupied building. Below: The ornate, Renaissance-style City Hall.*

Vom Hafen erstreckt sich die elegante Heerengracht (gegenüber) in Richtung Berg; halbwegs wird sie zur Adderleystraße, Hauptgeschäftsstraße der Stadt. Links: Die mächtigen Steinmauern vom Kastell; die Festung, der Bau war 1676 beendet, ist das älteste noch bewohnte Gebäude des Landes. Unten: Die im Stil der Renaissance gebaute, reich gezierte Stadthalle.

L'artère élégant Heerengracht (ci-contre) parcourt la ville, allant du port vers la montagne, changeant son nom en Rue Adderley– la principale voie commerciale de la ville–en mi-chemin. A gauche: Le château 'the Castle', une forteresse qui fut finie en 1676 et qui reste aujourd'hui le plus vieux bâtiment occupé en Afrique du Sud. Ci-dessous: L'hôtel de ville–le City Hall–en style renaissance fleuri.

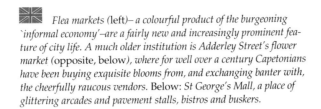 Flea markets (left)– a colourful product of the burgeoning 'informal economy'–are a fairly new and increasingly prominent feature of city life. A much older institution is Adderley Street's flower market (opposite, below), where for well over a century Capetonians have been buying exquisite blooms from, and exchanging banter with, the cheerfully raucous vendors. **Below:** St George's Mall, a place of glittering arcades and pavement stalls, bistros and buskers.

Neuerdings beleben immer mehr die bunten Trödelmärkte (links)–Ausdruck des 'unförmlichen Wirtschaftsektors'– das Stadtbild. Viel älter hingegen ist der Blumenmarkt (gegenüber, unten) in der Adderleystraße. Seit über hundert Jahren kaufen hier die Kapstädter herrliche Blumen, feilschen und scherzen mit den immer fröhlichen Verkäufern. Unten: St. George's Mall–die Fußgängerzone mit ihren glitzenden Arkaden, Verkaufsständen, Bistros und Straßenmusikanten.

Les marchés aux puces (à gauche)–le produit original d'une économie officieuse bourgeonnante–constituent une particularité assez nouvelle mais de plus en plus importante de la vie urbaine. Une institution bien plus établie est le marché aux fleurs de la Rue Adderley (ci-contre en bas), où depuis plus d'un siècle les habitants du Cap se procurent leurs fleurs magnifiques et badinent joyeusement avec les vendeurs bruyants et gais. Ci-dessous: Le St. George's Mall, un endroit garni de galeries resplendissantes, de kiosques et étalages, de bistros et de cabotins.

Below: *A dappled, tree-lined walkway, Government Avenue, flanks the South African Museum (opposite, above) as well as the Company's Garden, which was planted in the 1650s as a humble vegetable patch and has since become one of the country's most attractive and botanically interesting city parks. On the slopes of nearby Signal Hill is the historic Bo-Kaap suburb (opposite, below), home to much of the city's Islamic community.*

Unten: *Government Avenue, die von Bäumen gesäumte Allee, führt durch den 'Company's Garden', angelegt als Gemüsegarten in den 1650iger Jahren, aber heute einer der attraktivsten botanischen Stadtgärten. Das Südafrikanische Museum (gegenüber, oben) flankiert die Allee. Auf den nahen Hängen des Signal Hill erstreckt sich der historische Vorort 'Bo-Kaap' (gegenüber, unten) wo viele Angehöriges der islamischen Gemeinde wohnen.*

Ci-dessous: *L'Avenue du Gouvernement, bordée d'arbres et voisine du Musée Sud Africain (ci-contre, au-dessus). Les Jardins de la Compagnie, plantés en 1650 comme humble jardin potager et aujourd'hui l'un des parcs urbains des plus séduisants et botaniquement intéressants du pays. Sur les pentes du Signal Hill (la colline du signal) proche de la ville, se trouve le faubourg historique 'Bo-Kaap', où réside la plupart de la communauté islamique de la ville.*

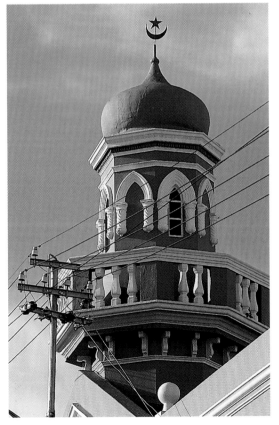

Above: *Sunset view from the mountain's summit; the building is the cable station. There are several well-trodden paths leading up the steep slopes, though most visitors choose to take the cable car (opposite, above). At the top there are observation sites, a restaurant (opposite, below), a souvenir shop, and short walks across the 'table', with splendid views of both coastlines.*

Oben: *Blick bei Sonnenuntergang vom Gipfel; sichtbar ist die Seilbahnstation. Zahlreiche, wohl betretene, steile Wanderwege führen bergauf, doch die meisten Besucher bevorzugen die Seilbahn (gegenüber, oben.) Hochoben gibt es Aussichtspunkte, ein Restaurant (gegenüber, unten), einen Andenkenladen und natürlich bieten sich kurze Spaziergänge über das Gipfelplateau an!*

Ci-dessus: *Coucher du soleil, au sommet de la montagne; l'immeuble du téléphérique. Plusieurs chemins battus vous mènent le long des pentes escarpées, bien que la plupart des visiteurs prennent le téléphérique (ci-contre, au-dessus). Au sommet on trouve des sites d'observation, un restaurant (ci-contre, en bas), une boutique de souvenirs et quelques promenades faciles sur 'la table' même!*

 The mountain viewed from the seafront at Bloubergstrand. On clear days its distinctive outline can be discerned 200 km out to sea, though the heights are often obscured by the `tablecloth', a spectacular continuum of clouds that billow over the rim to tumble down the massively precipitous northern faces.

Der Berg, von Bloubergstrand her gesehen. Bei klarem Wetter zeichnen sich seine unverkennbaren Kontouren vom Meer her in einer Entfernung von über 200 km ab. Wolken türmen sich oft über dem Gipfel, bedecken ihn mit einem breiten 'Tischtuch' und rollen dann die gewaltige, steile Nordseite des Berges herab.

Vue de la montagne à partir de la plage de Bloubergstrand. Par temps clair, la silhouette bien distinctive de la montagne se distingue de 200 km de distance sur l'océan, bien que sa hauteur se voile souvent derrière la 'nappe', un continuum spectaculaire de nuages s'ondoyant en cascades, descendant les faces-nord massivement précipitées.

🇬🇧 *Much of Cape Town's busy dockland area is now given over to leisure and pleasure.* **Opposite:** *Moorings at the Royal Cape Yacht Club.* **Right:** *Start of the famed Cape-to-Rio yacht race.* **Below:** *Governor's House, Robben Island, a short boat ride from the waterfront.*

🇩🇪 *Sport und Vergnügen haben heutzutage einen großen Teil des geschäftigen Hafens übernommen.* **Gegenüber:** *Vertäuung im Royal Cape Jachtklub.* **Rechts:** *Start des berühmten Wettsegelns von 'Kap nach Rio'.* **Unten:** *Das Haus des Goeverneur's auf Robben Island, eine kurze Bootsfahrt von Hafen entfernt.*

🇫🇷 *Une grande partie du quartier des docks de la Ville du Cap vient d'être rénovée pour des besoins de loisirs et de plaisirs.* **Ci-contre:** *Les amarrages du Royal Cape Yacht Club.* **A droite:** *Au départ de la cèlébre course de yachts 'Cap à Rio'.* **Ci-dessous:** *La maison du gouverneur, sur Robben Island, qui reste une traversée courte des quais.*

The energy and ambience of the waterfront now rival Table Mountain as the Cape Peninsula's premier attraction. Above: *Alfresco dining at the docks.* Opposite, above: *Generations of visitors have used the 'penny ferry' to see the sights.* Opposite, below: *A fishing trawler on tourist duty.*

Das Hafenviertel rivalisiert mit dem Tafelberg als Touristen-attraktion in der Kaphalbinsel. Oben: *Al fresko Essen im Hafen.* Gegenüber, oben: *Seit Generationen benutzen Besucher die Penny-Fähre für Rundfahrten.* Gegenüber, unten: *Ein Trawler wird zum Ausflugsboot.*

Ces jours-ci, le nouveau quartier des docks peut rivaliser avec la Montagne de la Table comme attraction vedette de la Péninsule du Cap. Ci-contre, ci-dessus: *Des générations de touristes et visiteurs ont pris le 'penny ferry' pour voir les endroits célèbres.* Ci-contre, en-dessous: *Un chalutier en randonnée touristique.*

Cape Town harbour's Victoria and Alfred basins –now a fantasia of charmingly remodelled buildings, of promenades and squares, hotels, shops, pubs, eateries, fish and flea markets, museums and marinas–have brought city and sea together again in happy reunion. Right: *A quayside music-maker.*

Bei den Victoria und Alfred Hafenbecken bringen geschmackvoll und reizend sanierte Gebäude, Fußwege, öffentliche Plätze, Hotels, Geschäfte, Wirtshäuser, Fisch- und Trödelmärkte, Museen und Jachtbassins–wieder Leben in das Hafenviertel. Hier haben sich Stadt und See gefunden. Rechts: *Ein Musikant am Hafendamm.*

Les bassins Victoria et Alfred au port de la Ville du Cap–toute une fantaisie de bâtiments exquisement remodelés, de promenades, allées et places, d'hôtels et de boutiques, de bistros, pubs, restaurants, de marchés de poissons et de marchés aux puces, de musées et de ports de plaisance–ont enfin de nouveau et heureusement réuni ville et mer. A droite: *Un musicien des quais.*

Focal point of the waterfront is the Pier Head speciality shopping complex and its 15 restaurants. On the drawing board are a world-class oceanarium, a yacht basin, and a waterway leading into the city. Opposite and above: *Harbour lights*. Left: *A dockside bistro*.

Mittelpunkt im Hafenviertel ist das Einkaufszentrum am 'Pier Head', der Hafendamm mit seinem vielen Fachgeschäften und 15 Restaurants; geplant sind ein erstklassiges Ozeanarium, Jachthafen und ein Kanal zur Stadt. Gegenüber und oben: *Hafenlichter*. Links: *Ein Hafenlokal*.

Le foyer social du 'Waterfront': le 'Pier Head', un centre commercial comblé de boutiques et magasins de spécialités, avec 15 restaurants. Prévus sous peu sont également: un aquarium d'eau de mer d'intérêt universel, un bassin pour yachts et un cours d'eau menant au centre-ville. Ci-contre et ci-dessus: *Les lumières du port*. A gauche: *Un bistro des quais*.

Cape Town's Atlantic seaboard is a magnet for the holidaymaker. Right, above: *The Sea Point promenade*. Right and below: *Mouille Point and its historic lighthouse*. Opposite: *The white sands of Clifton*.

Kapstadts atlantische Küste lockt den Urlauber. Rechts, oben: *Die Promenade in Sea Point*. Rechts und unten: *Mouille Point und der historische Leuchtturm*. Gegenüber: *Der weiße Sand von Clifton*.

Le littoral atlantique de la Ville du Cap attire beaucoup de touristes. A droite, au-dessus: *La Promenade à Sea Point*. A droite et ci-dessous: *Mouille Point et son phare historique*. Ci-contre: *Les plages blanches de Clifton*.

The Cape Riviera

Below and opposite, below: *Popular among sun-worshippers are the silky, bleached sands of Clifton's Fourth Beach and nearby Camps Bay.* Left: *Treasures of the sea on sale along the scenic coastal drive.* Opposite, above: *Camps Bay, with two of the towering Twelve Apostles buttresses in the background.*

Unten, und gegenüber, unten: *Cliftons Fourth Beach und der nahe Strand von Camps Bay sind bei den Sonnenanbetern beliebt.* Links: *Schätze aus dem Meer auf der malerischen Küstenstraße zum Verkauf angeboten.* Gegenüber, oben: *Zwei der 'Twelve Apostles' ("Zwölf Aposteln") ragen hoch über Camps Bay.*

Ci-dessous et ci-contre, en-dessous: *La Quatrième Plage de Clifton et Camps Bay, les lieux préférés des adorateurs du soleil.* A gauche: *Des trésors de la mer, en vente le long de la route côtière spectaculaire.* Ci-contre, au-dessus: *Camps Bay avec en arrière-plan deux des gigantesques Douze Apôtres en contreforts.*

Above and opposite, above: *The winding, scenically spectacular western coastal route from the city brings you to the exclusive little seaside village of Llandudno, set beneath a peak called Little Lion's Head. Over the hill is Hout Bay (opposite, below), definitely one of the most attractive of the Cape's fishing harbours.*

Oben und gegenüber, oben: *Von der Stadt herkommend, führt die malerische, bergaufwindende Küstenstraße zum hübschen Vorort Llundudno, im Schatten des Little Lion's Head (Kleiner Löwenkopf) gelegen. Hout Bay (gegenüber, unten) liegt hinter dem Berg und ist wohl der reizvollste Fischereihafen im Kapland.*

Au-dessus et ci-contre au-dessus: *La route en lacets scéniquement spectaculaire, allant de la ville tout le long de la côte ouest, vous conduit vers le petit village balnéaire exclusif de Llandudno, au pied du pic de montagne La Tête du Petit Lion. Passé la colline se trouve Hout Bay (ci-contre, ci-dessous), un port de pêche des plus séduisants au Cap.*

Above: *Hobie Cats at Hout Bay. The village nestles in a beautiful, forested valley; its picturesque harbour is the hub of the Peninsula's rock lobster fleet. From here, the road south takes you along the dramatic Chapman's Peak drive* (opposite, below) *to the white, sandy stretches of Noordhoek* (opposite, above).

Oben: *Hobie Cats in Hout Bay. Das Dorf liegt in einem herrlichen, grünen Tal; in seinem Hafen laufen die Hummerboote ein, und von hier führt die Küstenstraße in südlicher Richtung über den spektakulären Bergpass Chapman's Peak* (gegenüber, unten) *zum großen, weißen Strand von Noordhoek* (gegenüber, oben).

Ci-dessus: *Les Hobie Cats (catamarans) à Hout Bay. Le village est blotti dans une belle vallée couverte de forêts; son port pittoresque est le centre de pêche de la langouste dans la Péninsule. De là, la route serpente autour du Chapman's Peak* (ci-contre, en bas) *jusqu'aux sables blancs de Noordhoek* (ci-contre, en haut).

The massive prominence of Cape Point–its cliffs fall almost sheer for 300 metres–is at the Peninsula's southern extremity. It is off this headland that sightings of The Flying Dutchman, *the phantom ship destined to sail the seas until Doomsday, have been recorded.* Below: *Nearby Diaz Beach.*

Die Kapspitze–jäh stürzen die Felswände über 300 m in die Tiefe–ist der südlichste Zipfel der Halbinsel. Von hier hat man das Geisterschiff Der Fliegende Holländer *gesichtet, verdammt dazu, das Kap bis zum Jüngsten Tag zu umschiffen.* Unten: *Der nahe Dias-Strand.*

La Pointe du Cap–dont les falaises se dressent sur une hauteur de presque 300 mètres–représente l'extrémité sud de la Péninsule. De ce promontoire on aurait vu, à plusieurs reprises, Le Hollandais Volant, *ce vaisseau fantôme, destiné à naviguer les mers jusqu'à la fin du monde.* En bas: *La plage Dias toute proche.*

🇬🇧 *Much of the Peninsula's southern segment has been set aside as the Cape of Good Hope nature reserve, famed for its rich variety of flowering plants; for its often overfamiliar baboons (opposite, below) and, among scuba-divers (below), for its marine life. Of historical interest are the Diaz Cross (left), a monument to the great Portuguese navigator; and the small museum (opposite, above).*

🇩🇪 *Ein großes Gebiet der Halbinsel wird vom Naturschutzpark 'Cape of Good Hope' (Kap der Guten Hoffnung) eingenommen. Der Park ist bekannt für die Vielfältigkeit der Blumen, die oft zu aufdringlichen Paviane (gegenüber, unten) und beliebt bei den Tauchern (unten) wegen seiner Tiefseefauna. Geschichtlich interessant sind das Dias-Kreuz (links), das den berühmten portugiesischen Seefahrer ehrt, sowie auch das kleine Museum (gegenüber, oben).*

🇫🇷 *Le segment sud de la Péninsule a en grande partie été retenu en tant que Réserve Naturelle du Cap de Bonne Espérance, surtout connue pour son exceptionnelle diversité de plantes fleuries, ses babouins souvent trop effrontés (ci-contre, en bas) et la beauté de sa faune et flore marine, très prudemment gardée par les plongeurs sous-marins (ci-dessous). Ses monuments historiques: La Croix Dias (à gauche), pour honorer ce grand navigateur Portugais et le tout petit musée (ci-contre, en haut).*

The Peninsula's eastern shoreline is lapped by the warm, intensely blue waters of False Bay. Among the popular and rather charmingly old-fashioned vacation venues here are St James (above), and Muizenberg (left) which is renowned for its magnificent beach. Simon's Town (opposite), steeped in naval tradition, is the most prominent of the coastal centres.

An der östlichen Küste der Halbinsel, leckt warmes, tiefblaues Meereswasser den Strand. Zu den beliebten und reizvoll altmodischen Ferienorten gehören St. James (oben), und Muizenberg (links) mit seinem prachtvollen Strand. Simon's Town (gegenüber) traditionsreiche Hafenstadt, ist der bekannteste Küstenort.

Le rivage-est de la Péninsule est batillé par les eaux tièdes, d'un bleu vif, de False Bay. Les lieux de villégiature les plus en vogue de ce côté sont les charmants et doucement surannés St James (ci-dessus)–et Muizenberg (à gauche), célèbre pour sa plage magnifique. Simon's Town avec sa tradition navale invétérée (ci-contre), est le plus important des centres côtiers.

For sheer scenic beauty, few parts of the Cape–indeed, of Africa–can compare with the fertile valley of Constantia, noted for its vistas, its oak-lined drives and its historic wine estates, of which Groot Constantia (the homestead is shown below; the cellar at right) and Klein Constantia (opposite) are the best known.

Gibt es im Kapland, in Afrika, wohl eine landschaftlich schönere Gegend als Constantia? Dieses fruchtbare, wasserreiche Tal mit seinen einmaligen Aussichten, von Eichen gesäumten Fahrwegen, historischen Weingütern, unter denen Groot Constantia (das Gutshof ist unten abgebildet, mit Weinkeller rechts) und Klein Constantia (gegenüber) zu den bekanntesten zählen, kennt keinesgleichen.

Peu nombreux sont les coins du Cap–et même de l'Afrique–qui puissent rivaliser en pure beauté scénique avec la vallée bien arrosée, fertile de Constantia, célèbre pour ses perspectives splendides, ses allées plantées de vieux chênes et ses propriétés vinicoles historiques, dont Groot Constantia (ci-dessous: le homestead; à droite: la cave) et Klein Constantia (ci-contre) sont les mieux connus.

One of the world's most important botanic centres is Kirstenbosch, whose gardens extend over the south-eastern slopes of the Table Mountain range. Here some 9 000 indigenous flowering plants are cultivated, among them a wealth of proteas (opposite, below).

Kirstenbosch, an den süd-östlichen Hängen des Tafelberges, zählt zu den wichtigsten botanischen Gärten der Welt. Hier werden über 9 000 einheimische Pflanzen, darunter auch unzählige Proteen, (gegenüber, unten) kultiviert.

Kirstenbosch, un des centres botaniques les plus importants au monde: ses jardins s'étendent sur l'inclinaison sud-est de la Montagne de la Table. On y cultive 9 000 variétés de plantes fleuries du pays, parmi lesquelles toute une profusion de protées (ci-contre, en bas).

Much of the land below Table Mountain's eastern heights was bequeathed to the nation by the 19th-century financier and politician Cecil Rhodes. The land embraces, among much else, his memorial (below), designed in grandly classical style by Sir Herbert Baker, together with its tearoom (above); the university campus (opposite, above); and historic Mostert's Mill (opposite, below), built in 1796.

Ein großes Gebiet an den östlichen Berghängen des Tafelberges ist eine Schenkung des Politikers und Finanziers des 19ten Jahrhunderts, Cecil Rhodes, an die Nation. Hier würdigt ihn sein Denkmal (unten) im großartig klassischem Stil; auch die Teestube (oben) und das Hochschulgelände der Universität (gegenüber, oben) und die historische Mostert Mühle (gegenüber, unten) gebaut in 1796, liegen hier.

Une importante partie des terres sur l'élévation est de la Montagne Table fut léguée à la Nation par Cecil Rhodes, un financier-politicien du 19ième siècle. Le domaine englobe, entre beaucoup d'autres, son monument commémoratif (ci-dessous), conçu en splendide style classique, un salon de thé (ci-dessus), le campus universitaire (ci-contre, en haut) et le moulin historique 'Mostert's Mill' (ci-contre, en bas), construit en 1796.

Oldest and arguably the most attractive town in the western Cape hinterland–commonly known as the Winelands– is Stellenbosch, founded in 1679. Right: *Dorp Street, an architectural treasure house.* Above: *The historic general dealer's shop.* Opposite, above: *Part of the university campus.* Opposite, below: *Open-air concert at Oude Libertas.*

Zweifellos die älteste und wohl auch schönste Stadt im westlichen Hinterland ist Stellenbosch, gegründet in 1679. Rechts: *Dorp Street (Dorfstraße), ein architektonischer Juwel.* Oben: *Der historische Krämerladen.* Gegenüber, oben: *Teil der Hochschulanlage der Universität.* Gegenüber, unten: *Konzert in der Freilichtbühne Oude Libertas.*

Stellenbosch, fondée en 1679, est la plus ancienne ville et tout probablement aussi la plus attirante de l'arrière-pays du Cap Occidental–qu'on appelle la Région Vignoble. A droite: *Dorp Street (la Rue du Village), un trésor architectural.* Ci-dessus: *L'épicerie-droguerie historique.* Ci-contre, en haut: *Un coin du campus universitaire.* Ci-contre, en bas: *Un concert en plein air à Oude Libertas.*

Opposite, below: *Vineyard panorama. Altogether, some 5 000 Cape grape-growers cultivate over 300 million vines to produce generally good and sometimes superb wines.* Opposite, above, and below: *Boschendal estate's homestead and picnic area.* Left: *Picking waterblommetjies (`water-flowers'), the ingredient of a delicious bredie, or stew.*

Gegenüber, unten: *Weingarten Panorama. Etwa 5 000 Winzer kultivieren über 300 Millionen Weinstöcke, und produzieren ausnahmslos gute, teilweise hervorragende Weine.* Gegenüber, oben und unten: *Das Weingut Boschendal mit Picknick-platz.* Links: *Bei der Ernte von waterblommetjies (Wasserblumen), Zutat für einen köstlichen Eintopf, oder 'bredie'.*

Ci-contre, en bas: *Vue panoramique des vignobles. 5 000 vignerons du Cap en tout cultivent plus de 300 millions de vignes qui produisent des vins généralement bons et parfois superbes.* Ci-contre, en haut et en bas: *Le domaine de Boschendal, son homestead et son coin pique-nique.* A gauche: *La cueillette de 'Waterblommetjies' (fleurs de fontaine), l'ingrédient principal d'un des fameux plats-ragoûts délicieux, qu'on appelle ici 'bredie'.*

Right: *The attractive, lush green Franschhoek valley. The memorial in the distance commemorates the arrival, in 1688, of a small party of French Huguenot refugees and the role they played in developing the Winelands region.* Above: *Visitors to the valley enjoy afternoon tea.* Top: *A country hotel near Paarl.*

Rechts: *Das grüne, hübsche Tal von Franschhoek. In der Ferne sieht man das Hugenotten Denkmal, im Andenken an die kleine Gruppe französischer Flüchtlinge gebaut, die 1688 ins Land kamen und zur Entwicklung des Weinbaus beitragen haben.* Oben: *Besucher im Tal genießen ihren Nachmittagstee.* Oben: *Ein ländliches Hotel bei Paarl.*

A droite: *La charmante vallée verte de Franschhoek. Le monument commémoratif au loin célèbre l'arrivée, en 1688, d'un petit groupe de réfugiés Huguenots français et le rôle qu'ils ont joué dans le développement de la région vignoble.* Ci-dessus: *Des visiteurs de la vallée savourent leur goûter.* En haut: *Un hôtel de campagne près de Paarl.*

The coastal region beyond the mountains is famed for its wild flowers (below), most of them species of fynbos, a primitive and botanically fascinating heath-like type of vegetation. Opposite: Gordon's Bay, a charming resort village and fishing harbour that is popular among yachtsmen and vacationing families.

Das Küstengebiet jenseits der Berge ist für seine Feldblumen (unten) bekannt, die hauptsächlich zum 'Fynbos' gehören, eine botanisch faszinierende, der Heide ähnlichen Vegetation. Gegenüber: Gordon's Bay, ein reizender Ferienort und Fischereihafen, beliebt bei Seglern und Familien auf Urlaub.

La région littorale au-delà des montagnes est renommée pour ses fleurs sauvages (ci-dessous), surtout des espèces de 'fynbos', un genre de bruyère primitive et botaniquement fascinante. Ci-contre: Gordon's Bay, un charmant village balnéaire avec un port de pêche populaire parmi les yachtsmen et les vacanciers.

*Struik Publishers (Pty) Ltd
(a member of Struik New Holland Publishing (Pty) Ltd)
80 McKenzie Street, Cape Town 8001*

Reg. No.: 54/00965/07

First published 1993

4 6 8 10 9 7 5

*Text © Peter Joyce 1993
Photographs © individual photographers and/or
their agents as follows:*

Daryl Balfour *p 42 (bottom), p 44 (top), p 48
(top left) [ABPL];* **Anthony Bannister** *p 26;*
Gerald Cubitt *p 8, p 11 (bottom), p 14 (top),
p 33 (bottom), p 36 (top), p 37, p 45;* **Walter Knirr**
*front cover (also inset bottom) and back cover, p 2
[Photo Access], p 5, p 12 [Photo Access],
p 15 (bottom), p 20 (top), p 24, p 28 (top), p 29,
p 32 (top and bottom), p 34 (top and bottom), p 46
(top), p 47;* **Nicola Newman** *p 18 (top), p 19 (bottom);*
Struik Image Library *front cover (inset top),
p 4 (top), p 6 (bottom), p 7 (bottom), p 9, p 10 (top),
p 11 (top right), p 14 (bottom), p 15 (top), p 16, p 17,
p 18 (bottom), p 19 (top), p 22 (bottom), p 23 (bottom),
p 25, p 28 (bottom), p 30 (bottom), p 31, p 33 (top), p 35,
p 36 (bottom), p 38 (bottom), pp 40/41, p 42 (top),
p 43 (top), p 44 (bottom), p 46 (bottom),
p 48 (top right and bottom);* **Mark van
Aardt** *p 4 (bottom), p 6 (top), p 10 (bottom),
p 20 (centre and bottom), p 30 (top), p 38 (top), p 39
(top and bottom);* **Hein von Hörsten** *p 1 [ABPL];*
Patrick Wagner *p 21, p 22 (top),
p 23 (top), p 27 (top) [all Photo Access];* **Keith Young**
p 27 (bottom), p 43 (bottom).
ABPL = Anthony Bannister Photo Library

*French translation by Hilde Poulter-Kooyman
German translation by Ursula Stevens
Designed by Alix Gracie
Typesetting by Struik DTP, Cape Town
Reproduction by Unifoto (Pty) Ltd, Cape Town
Printed and bound by Kyodo Printing Co
(Singapore) Pte Ltd*

ISBN 1 86825 434 8

🏴 Top: *The rugged Walker Bay shore near Hermanus, a largish resort town much favoured by weekend holidaymakers. The bay plays wintertime host to giant southern right whales (above, left), whose annual appearance is announced by the town's `whale crier' (above, right).*

🏴 *Die zerklüftete Walker Bay Küste bei Hermanus, ein etwas größerer und beliebter Ferienort für Wochenendler. Im Winter tummeln sich riesige Wale (oben, links) in der Bucht. Der öffentliche Ausrufer (oben, rechts) kündigt alljährlich ihr Kommen an.*

🏴 Au-dessus: *Le rivage de Walker Bay, près de Hermanus, un centre de villégiature assez important et très voulu parmi les vacanciers du weekend. La baie joue le rôle d'hôte d'hiver pour les baleines franches géantes du sud (ci-dessus, à gauche), dont l'apparition annuelle est annoncée par le 'crieur municipal de baleines' (ci-dessus, à droite).*